Active Reader's Practice Book

PROGRAM DESIGNER AND GENERAL EDITOR

Kylene Beers, Ed.D.

UNIVERSITY OF HOUSTON

ELEMENTS OF
Literature
FIRST COURSE

MiniReads
MiniRead Practice Activity Worksheets
Selection Practice Activity Worksheets
Additional Practice Graphic Organizers

D1279431

Charlene
Wilson

HOLT, RINEHART AND WINSTON
Harcourt Brace & Company

Austin • New York • Orlando • Atlanta • San Francisco • Boston • Dallas • Toronto • London

Staff Credits

Director: Mescal Evler

Manager of Editorial Operations: Bill Wahlgren

Managing Editor: Marie Price

Executive Editor: Patricia A. McCambridge

Project Editor: Victoria Moreland

Component Editors: Pamela Thompson, Scott Hall, Tracy DeMont

Editorial Staff: *Assistant Editor,* Chi Nguyen; *Copyediting Manager,* Michael Neibergall; *Senior Copyeditor,* Mary Malone; *Copyeditors,* Joel Bourgeois, Gabrielle Field, Suzi A. Hunn, Jane Kominek, Millicent Ondras, Theresa Reding, Désirée Reid, Kathleen Scheiner; *Editorial Coordinators,* Marcus Johnson, Mark Holland, Jill O'Neal, Janet Riley; *Support Staff,* Lori De La Garza; *Word Processors,* Ruth Hooker, Margaret Sanchez, Gail Coupland

Research and Development: Joan Burditt

Permissions: Tamara A. Blanken, Ann B. Farrar

Design: *Art Director, Book & Media Design,* Joe Melomo

Prepress Production: Beth Prevelige, Simira Davis, Sergio Durante

Media Production: *Production Manager,* Kim A. Scott; *Production Coordinator,* Belinda Barbosa; *Production Supervisor,* Nancy Hargis

Manufacturing Coordinator: Michael Roche

Printed in the United States of America

ISBN 0-03-064576-X

234567 22 02 01

Reading Skills and Strategies

TABLE OF CONTENTS

Additional Practice 117

To the Student

This *Reading Skills and Strategies: Active Reader's Practice Book* is a resource for you, the student, to use in conjunction with your teacher's *Reading Skills and Strategies* binder. In this booklet, you will find materials made specifically for you: texts and activity worksheets that you can write on, draw on, and mark up in any way that helps you to become a more active, involved reader.

This *Reading Skills and Strategies: Active Reader's Practice Book* is designed to be used with your *Elements of Literature* anthology. In this book, you will find four different kinds of reading materials and practice activities that will help you to become a more confident user of reading strategies: MiniReads, MiniRead Practice Activity Worksheets, Selection Practice Activity Worksheets, and Additional Practice graphic organizers (for use with particular reading strategies).

MiniReads are short, high-interest reading selections that will help you to develop and practice specific reading skills and strategies. In the margins of every MiniRead, there is ample room for you to write your own notes and comments as you read. You can also mark the MiniReads in any way that you find helpful, highlighting important passages or circling words and phrases that seem especially significant. Each MiniRead is followed by a **MiniRead Practice Activity Worksheet** that gives you an opportunity to apply the skills and strategies you have learned in that particular MiniRead lesson. Many of the activities on these worksheets involve group or partner work, but you or your teacher can adjust and customize the lessons in any ways that you wish.

In addition to the MiniReads and their accompanying MiniRead Practice Activity Worksheets, you will also find **Selection Practice Activity Worksheets**. These worksheets accompany specific selections in your *Elements of Literature* anthology, giving you opportunities to apply the reading skills and strategies you have learned through the MiniRead to specific selections in your textbook. The reading skill presented in a Selection Practice Activity Worksheet will be the same Reading Skills and Strategies (RSS) skill that appears on the selection's Before You Read page in your Pupil's Edition. Selection Practice Activity Worksheets include a variety of interesting, interactive tasks that will help you build reading skills and strategies that you can transfer to any kind of reading that you do, whether it be reading your school textbooks, enjoying an entertaining novel, or reading a magazine for information.

Finally, at the back of this book, in a section called Additional Practice, you'll find graphic organizers that you can use to help you with various reading strategies that you may find yourself using again and again, such as Somebody Wanted But So, It Says . . . I Say, and Think-Aloud, among others. You will find it helpful to use these graphic organizers in a variety of reading situations, both inside and outside of class.

Active readers interact with texts in a variety of ways. This booklet provides you with opportunities to take notes, mark up texts, and complete reading skills and strategies activities that will build your reading skills and help to make you a more confident, engaged reader.

Joan Burditt has a Master's Degree in Education with a specialization in reading. She has taught in regular classrooms as well as in programs for struggling readers. Currently a program development consultant, she has written for educational publishers and magazines on a wide range of subjects.

Richard Cohen is an educational writer and editor as well as a novelist. He has written a college creative-writing textbook, *Writer's Mind: Crafting Fiction*, and the novels *Domestic Tranquillity, Don't Mention the Moon*, and *Say You Want Me*. A graduate of the University of Michigan, he has taught creative writing at the University of Wisconsin, Madison.

Ed Combs is a freelance writer and editor. Combs graduated from St. Edward's University in Austin, Texas, and has written and edited for educational publishers, standardized testing companies, magazines, and newspapers for fifteen years. He taught English and basketball to at-risk students in Atlanta, Georgia.

Tom Dowe graduated from Yale College and received an M.A. in English and American Literature from The University of Texas at Austin. He has written for *Wired, Mother Jones, The New York Times Magazine*, and many web-based magazines. His poetry and prose have appeared in numerous literary journals. He is currently writing a biography of the poet Kenneth Koch.

Tracy Duncan is an artist, writer, and editor. She graduated from The University of Texas at Austin and has written and edited for textbook publishers, standardized testing companies, magazines, and newspapers for fourteen years. She served as an Artist-in-Residence for the Atlanta Project.

Corinne Greiner is a freelance writer. She attended the Iowa Writers' Workshop and the Radcliffe Publishing Institute on fellowships. A winner of the Bank of America Award for Young Writers, she was also a finalist for the Annie Dillard Award in Nonfiction and a nominee for the Pushcart Prize.

Patty Kolar taught secondary English, journalism, and reading for ten years. A Phi Beta Kappa graduate of The University of Texas at Austin, she was curriculum coordinator for an after-school child-care agency and currently works in the research and curriculum department of a leading educational publisher.

Mary Beth Mader has worked as an advertising copywriter and is currently a philosophy instructor. She holds a Ph.D. in Philosophy. She was a 1992 recipient of the French government's Chateaubriand Fellowship and is the translator of Luce Irigaray's *The Forgetting of Air in Martin Heidegger*.

Mimi Mayer received an M.F.A. in Creative Writing from the University of Michigan, where she lectured in composition and rhetoric from 1990–1993. Her work has been recognized with twelve national and regional awards from such organizations as the Council for the Advancement and Support of Education, the International Association of Business Communicators, and the Michigan Press Association. A published poet, Mayer has received fellowships from the Cranbook and the Aspen Writing Foundations.

Mary Olmstead, formerly a middle and high school English and French teacher, currently writes and edits for textbook publishing and testing companies. Past awards include National Endowment for the Humanities grants to study the teaching of literature, and grants from the French government and the U.S. Department of Defense for travel to France and the French Antilles to study the French culture.

Carrie Laing Pickett is a freelance writer, editor, and poet who writes and edits for educational publishers. She currently holds an M.F.A. in Poetry.

Mara Rockliff is a freelance writer and editor with a degree in American Civilization from Brown University. Currently residing in Louisa, Virginia, she has written several adaptations and other works for leading literature textbooks, as well as plays in a book titled *Plays for Classroom Performance.*

Nancy Shreve graduated from Kent State University in 1987 with a B.A. in English and Education. She has interned for Kent State University Press, taught middle school for six years, and is currently pursuing a degree in creative writing.

Adrienne Su studied at Harvard and the University of Virginia. She has had fellowships at Yaddo in Saratoga Springs, New York; the MacDowell Colony in Petersborough, New Hampshire; and the Fine Arts Work Center in Provincetown, Massachusetts. A former member of New York City's national poetry-slam team, she writes about contemporary poetry for the Scholastic magazine *Literary Cavalcade* and is the author of a book of poems, *Middle Kingdom* (1997).

Jeanne Claire van Ryzin received a B.A. in English from Columbia University and an M.A. in Creative Writing from The University of Texas at Austin. She has been a writing resident at the Ragdale Foundation in Lake Forest, Illinois. Her fiction has received a PEN Syndicated Fiction award, and she has been a finalist for the Hemingway Short Story Award and the Nelson Algren Award. She has written articles for *The New York Times* and other newspapers.

Lisa Weckerle received an M.A. in Performance Studies from The University of North Carolina at Chapel Hill and is currently pursuing a Ph.D. in Performance Studies. She has written for the *Berkeley Fiction Review* and the *New Writer's Showcase.* She has taught classes for both children and adults in children's theater, playwriting, and dramatic performance, and has directed over twenty-five plays for varied audiences.

Sarah Wolbach is a poet, educational writer, and editor. She received her M.F.A. in Poetry from the Texas Center for Writers at The University of Texas at Austin in 1996. The recipient of a post-graduate fellowship, she spent the 1996–1997 academic year in San Miguel de Allende, Mexico.

The Mystery of the Found Animal (FICTION) (page 1)

Ted and Martin find a small animal lying next to a fence. They assume it's dead, but they soon find out that, when it comes to dealing with small unidentified animals, it's sometimes better to leave well enough alone. A companion piece for **"Rikki-tikki-tavi"** (Pupil's Edition, page 2), Rudyard Kipling's tale of a brave mongoose, this piece is a quick, easy read.

The Secret Place (FICTION) (page 7)

We all need a place where we can be alone with our thoughts. Three intruders find out that the main character in this story is willing to go to any length to keep her secret place. This MiniRead is paired with **"Song of the Trees"** (Pupil's Edition, page 28), a story about a girl whose special place is in danger of being destroyed.

The Barn (FICTION) (page 13)

Two brothers are on their own. One of them has committed a crime; the other thinks he needs his brother in order to survive. Survival is also the theme in the companion selection **"Three Skeleton Key"** (Pupil's Edition, page 64), a story that's not for the faint of heart.

A New Life (HISTORICAL FICTION) (page 21)

What was life like for immigrants making their way to the United States in the 1800s? As this personal narrative shows, the overseas trip wasn't a luxury cruise. This MiniRead is paired with another personal narrative, an excerpt from *Homesick* (Pupil's Edition, page 104), about a child from the United States who lives in China.

Take a Look at Yourself (FICTION) (page 27)

Just as Ernesto in **Barrio Boy** (Pupil's Edition, page 124) endures sometimes uncomfortable changes, the character Jason in this MiniRead endures a great transformation—or, actually, two transformations. Jason changes physically when his genie makes him two inches tall. He changes internally when he discovers how scary things can be when you're the size of a thumb.

Word Up—or Down? (NONFICTION) (page 33)

Why do friends *hang out* instead of *hang in*? Why is it nice to be called *cool* but awful to be called *cold*? This playful article describes how confusing the English language can be. In **"Names/Nombres,"** the companion selection (Pupil's Edition, page 144), Julia Alvarez describes how the richness of languages gives the members of her family multiple names.

The Princess and the Amphibian (FAIRY TALE) (page 41)

This princess has a hard time staying out of trouble. Having promised a frog she will marry him, she finds herself trying to wiggle out of her commitment. Her parents, the king and queen, insist that she follow through with her promise. The frog doesn't help her a bit in this humorous fairy tale with a twist. Pair this MiniRead with another "tale with a twist," O. Henry's **"After Twenty Years"** (Pupil's Edition, page 192).

What Are You Saying? (FICTION) (page 49)

Do you say *soda* or *pop*? Where is your *water closet*? Did it just *sprinkle*, or was it a *frog-strangler*? Sometimes communication can be a problem, as the characters in this MiniRead learn. The story is a companion piece to **"The No-Guitar Blues"** (Pupil's Edition, page 216), in which the main character, Fausto, has a few problems getting the guitar of his dreams.

Success Story (PLAY) (page 59)

The poignant teleplay *Brian's Song* (Pupil's Edition, page 273), about the deep friendship between Gale Sayers and Brian Piccolo, has long been a favorite of both football fans and those who know nothing about sports. Its companion MiniRead, "Success Story," tells the story of two brothers whose relationship on and off the basketball court also teaches us something about brotherhood and friendship.

Project Salamander (SCIENCE FICTION) (page 65)

Cause-and-effect relationships affect us as much as the air we breathe affects us. "Project Salamander" takes an ironic look at complex causes and effects in the environment. Its companion piece is **"User Friendly"** (Pupil's Edition, page 356), in which we discover that our relationships with technology may be more complex than we think.

Cos Gives It Up (NONFICTION) (page 73)

This article explores Bill Cosby's personal and financial commitment to education. This essay is a companion piece for **"The Only Girl in the World for Me"** (Pupil's Edition, page 386), an autobiographical essay by Cosby himself.

The Labors of Jermaine (FICTION) (page 95)

Jermaine is worried about keeping his grades up while juggling an after-school job. Although his problems are more run-of-the-mill than those of Hercules in the companion selection, **"The Labors of Hercules"** (Pupil's Edition, page 540), the labor seems just as intense—and the stakes seem just as high when Jermaine is forced to wrestle with an ethical dilemma.

Seeing Is Believing (FICTION) (page 109)

Alex can't believe what she has just seen her best friend Bobbi do. Stealing is bad enough, but taking money from your closest friend's father is as low as you can get. Alex struggles with how to deal with this breach of trust. Oni in **"Oni and the Great Bird"** (Pupil's Edition, page 628) encounters a very different struggle, one in which he's fighting for his life.

MiniReads, MiniRead Practice Activity Worksheets, and Selection Practice Activity Worksheets

The Mystery of the Found Animal

1   At first, all Ted and Martin could see was a small mound of black fur. It was some kind of small animal, about the size of a cat, lying next to a barbed-wire fence post. The two six-year-old boys stood back and watched for several minutes, but the furry mound didn't move. Ted whistled loudly. There was no response.

2   Ted turned to Martin. "It's dead. Let's bury it."

3   "I don't know," Martin said slowly. "Maybe it's just pre-tending to be dead. I think you have to listen for its heartbeat to know if it really *is* dead."

4   "Well, to listen to its heartbeat we'll have to touch it. Let's get closer."

5   "Hey, I'm not going to touch it," Martin replied. "We don't even know what it is. Anyway, it might have rabies or something."

6   Suddenly, the animal began to move slightly. It twitched its small nose. Then its front right paw moved up toward its face as if it were trying to wipe something off its mouth. It lifted its long, bushy black tail a few inches off the ground, but the effort seemed too much for the animal.

7   "Look!" Martin said in a whisper. "It *is* alive! But it's barely moving. It must be really hurt."

8   "Let's get it to my house. First we've got to get something to carry it in. There might be something in my garage. Come on!"

9   The boys ran across the field to Ted's house. They went into the garage, which was dark and smelled like paint and car oil. The boys left the door open for some light and began looking around. "Here!" Martin yelled after he spotted an old box.

10   "We can put this inside it," Ted said, holding up an old blanket. He thought the wounded animal might prefer a little soft padding.

11   The boys gathered up their supplies and ran back to the barbed-wire fence. The animal had not moved since the boys were last there. Now that the boys had moved closer to the animal, they noticed that the fur on its belly was all caked with dried blood. "It must have gotten caught on the barbed

ELEMENTS OF LITERATURE

wire," Ted said. "That's why I hate these fences."

12 "Do you think it's safe to pick it up?" Martin asked.

13 "I think it's okay if we're careful," Ted replied. "Besides, it's not very big, and it looks too hurt to try and fight us."

14 "Sometimes animals attack when they're hurt," Martin pointed out. "It might have claws."

15 "So you just want to leave it here to die?" Ted asked.

16 "I guess not," Martin admitted. "But maybe we should get someone to help us."

17 "If you're scared, I guess I'll just have to do it myself." Ted carefully started moving closer to the wounded animal.

18 At that moment, a woman's voice called out behind them.

19 "Boys! Get away from there right now!"

20 Suddenly, the small animal raised its head and shook it as though it had just awakened from a dream. Then it began to arch its bushy tail, raising it straight up off the ground and pulling it up over its back so that it nearly touched the back of its small black head. There was a narrow white stripe running straight down the middle of that furry tail.

21 Ted and Martin didn't notice the animal's tail because they were busy turning around to see who was shouting at them. Suddenly, though, they started coughing and choking. Their eyes began to burn and water. Worse yet, the air around them smelled more awful than anything they had ever smelled before.

22 The boys started running away from the small animal— and ran straight into Ted's mother.

23 "Oh, kids," she groaned. "Don't you know a skunk when you see one?"

24 Ted and Martin didn't see their mystery animal waddle off under the fence to get some peace and quiet so that it could heal. What they did see—when they could open their eyes a little—was the unforgettable expression on Ted's mother's face, and the way she held her nose closed with her fingers as she led the boys away from the scene of the skunk attack.

25 Later, after two tomato-juice baths, Ted and Martin were quite certain that they would know a skunk when they saw one again.

The Mystery of the Found Animal

SKILL MONITORING COMPREHENSION | **STRATEGY** THINK-ALOUD

Directions: Work with a partner to finish reading the MiniRead "The Mystery of the Found Animal" and make Think-Aloud comments. One partner should read aloud paragraphs 7–17, pausing to make comments, while the other partner uses a tally mark to identify the types of comments in the *Tally* column below. Then, switch roles and continue to the end of the MiniRead.

Think-Aloud Tally Sheet

Listener: _____

Think-Aloud Comments	Tally
Making predictions	
Picturing the text	
Making comparisons	
Identifying problems	
Fixing problems	
Making a comment	

ELEMENTS OF LITERATURE

Rikki-tikki-tavi

Directions: Work with a partner to read "Rikki-tikki-tavi" (Pupil's Edition, page 2) and make Think-Aloud comments. One partner should read aloud pages 4–10, pausing to make comments, while the other partner uses a tally mark to identify the types of comments the reader makes in the *Tally* column below. Then, switch roles and continue to the end of the selection.

Think-Aloud Tally Sheet

Listener:_____

Think-Aloud Comments	Tally
Making predictions	
Picturing the text	
Making comparisons	
Identifying problems	
Fixing problems	
Making a comment	

The Secret Place

1   Daisy couldn't wait for school to be out. She knew she'd have to run quickly out the front door or everyone would see where she was going. She tried to act like she wasn't impatient, like she wasn't about to burst waiting for that 3:30 bell to rrr-iii-nnn-ggg and for Miss Thompson to jump like she always did. Poor Miss Thompson always acted like she'd never heard the bell before. "Hurry, hurry, hurry," Daisy whispered to the long black hand on the face of the clock.

2   Finally, 3:30 arrived. Before the echo of the bell's clang had disappeared, Daisy was out of her seat, opening her locker, and heading toward the front door of the school. She was determined to make it to her secret place, the place where no one made fun of her, called her names, talked about her clothes, refused to sit by her at lunch, or ignored her between classes. She was determined to keep the place secret. She wouldn't share it with anyone, no matter what. What she didn't know was that Eddie, Bert, and Sammy were right behind her. They had seen her constant glances at the clock and had watched how quickly she ran out of the room.

3   "She's got a secret," Eddie said as the bell rang.

4   "Yeah. Let's find out what it is," Bert suggested.

5   "Don't let her see us," Sammy whispered as they threw their own books in their lockers.

6   Daisy didn't have a clue that the boys were behind her. She didn't see or hear them as they followed her down the hall, out the front door, through the busy schoolyard, and across the street. She did not know they were behind her as she jogged three blocks to the east, then turned left, and then jogged another four blocks. The boys were surprised when Daisy finally stopped at the edge of a huge lot that was filled with discarded tires and tall weeds. She ran through the weeds and clutter and finally stopped in front of a small shack that sat hidden at the back of the lot.

7   "Cool," Sammy exclaimed as the boys threw themselves onto their stomachs and let the tall grass and old tires hide them from Daisy's view. Daisy opened the door of the shack and went in.

8   "She's got a clubhouse."

9   "Not for long, she doesn't," Bert snickered.

10   The boys waited a long time for Daisy to come out, but she never did.

11   After a while Eddie said, "I'm getting hungry."

12   "And this grass itches," Bert said.

13   "Yeah, it itches," Sammy agreed.

14   "I think we'd be much more comfortable in our new clubhouse," Bert said.

15   "Yeah," Sammy nodded.

16   "But what if Daisy doesn't want us to use the shack as our clubhouse? What if she's decided it's her clubhouse?" Eddie asked.

17   "So what if she has?" Bert said. "There are three of us and only one of her."

18   "But I've heard she's pretty tough," Eddie said. "You know how she doesn't do things like other girls. Like coming here."

19   "So what?" Bert said. "I can handle her. She's just a girl."

20   Slowly the boys stood up and walked toward the shack door. When they got there, they called out Daisy's name. They could hear her singing softly, and they could smell a wonderful scent coming from inside the cabin.

21   "Hey, Daisy, you girl, come out. We want to talk to you," Bert called.

22   After a minute Daisy opened the door. She kept the door open and stood in the doorway staring at the boys. The boys looked inside and couldn't believe what they saw. Daisy had painted the walls a bright yellow. She had filled the shelves on the back wall with green plants. She had covered a table with a red-and-white-checked tablecloth that was filled with all shapes and sizes of candles. That's what smelled so good, the burning candles.

23   "So what do you want?" she asked.

24   "Uh, thanks for showing us this neat clubhouse and for getting it fixed up for us," Bert said. "But we'll be using it from now on."

25   He started toward the door, but she didn't move.

26   "This isn't your clubhouse. Go away," Daisy commanded.

27   "Now Daisy, be smart. You shouldn't be coming here all alone. It's not safe. So, we'll come instead and keep a good eye on your little clubhouse here," Bert said as he stepped closer.

28   "I don't need any boys taking care of my stuff," said Daisy, still not moving.

29   "Look, Daisy, we don't want any trouble, but you don't need this neat clubhouse all the time just for yourself," Bert explained. "Tell you what: We're fair guys, so we'll let you use it once a week, any day that you want it."

30   "I want it every day of the week because it's mine. I found it. I cleaned it. I painted it. It's mine," said Daisy.

31   "Well, it might have been yours, but now it's ours," Bert said, angry at this girl for not crying and running home like other girls would have done by now.

32   "Bert Johnson, you take one step closer to me and I'll push all these candles onto the floor of this old cabin. It will catch on fire so quickly you won't have time to get away before flames are everywhere." Daisy stepped back and picked up two burning candles from the table.

33   Sammy and Eddie looked at her and then at Bert. "Hey, man," Eddie said. "Remember what they call her at school, Crazy Daisy."

34   Bert stared at her for a moment. "I mean it, Bert," Daisy said. "I'd rather no one have this place than to hand it over to you just because you told me to."

35   Sammy and Eddie turned to go. "Come on, man, she's crazy. She'll burn it down and you with it," Eddie said. Bert watched the two burning candles that Daisy was holding, and he decided the boys were right.

36   "Yeah, she's crazy," he said, and the boys began to jog back toward their neighborhood.

37   Daisy watched them go and then put the candles down on the table. A small smile appeared on her face. They might think she was crazy, but she didn't care. This was her clubhouse. Hers.

The Secret Place

Directions: After you have read the MiniRead "The Secret Place," answer the questions in the following chart. You may have several comments under the *It Says* and *I Say* columns for each question, but you will only have one answer under the *And So* column for each question. The answer you write in the *And So* column is your inference. Continue your answers on another sheet of paper if necessary.

Question	It Says . . . + (What the text says)	I Say . . . = (My thoughts)	And So . . . (My inference)
1. How does Bert seem to feel about girls?			
2. Would Daisy have burned down the clubhouse?			
3. Who is braver, Daisy or Bert?			

ELEMENTS OF LITERATURE

Song of the Trees

Directions: After you have read "Song of the Trees" (Pupil's Edition, page 28), answer the questions in the following chart. (You may work with a partner.) You may have several comments under the *It Says* and *I Say* columns for each question but you will only have one answer under the *And So* column for each question. The answer you write in the final column is your generalization. Continue your answers on the back of this sheet if necessary.

Question	It Says . . . + (What the text says)	I Say . . . = (My thoughts)	And So . . . (My inference)	My Generalization
1. Why does Mr. Andersen think he has a right to chop down the Logans' trees?				
2. Why do the trees mean so much to Cassie and her family?				
3. Why does Mr. Logan (Papa) feel that it's better to blow up the forest than to allow Mr. Andersen to cut down the trees?				

The Barn

1   The barn was old. It had once been painted a bright red, but now it was faded, covered with peeling paint. It looked abandoned. Inside, though, the barn was spotless. Harnesses hung neatly from hooks. Hay bales were stacked carefully from the floor to the ceiling. Three lanterns stood at the end of a bench that was near the large doors. In the far back corner, there were two old mattresses, each covered with worn blankets. Between the mattresses stood an old crate that held two pairs of bluejeans, some shirts, socks, and a photograph of a woman holding a small boy as an older boy stood next to them.

2   Suddenly, the smaller side door to the barn flew open. Two people, one a boy about twelve years of age, the other a young man, rushed into the barn and slammed the door.

3   "I can't believe you did it again," the younger boy shouted, his face red with anger and streaked with tears. "You promised," he shouted.

4   "I'm sorry. It just happened. Now be quiet and let me think," his older brother hissed back as he lit a match to light a lantern. He carried the lantern back to the mattresses and set it on a nearby hay bale.

5   "You swore we could stay here, Tom. You swore there would be no more running."

6   "I said be quiet, Daniel," his brother hissed again. "Let me think."

7   The younger boy sat on his makeshift bed and wrapped his arms around his legs. He reached out to touch the photograph as if to assure himself that it was still there. *I wish I had more than this stupid picture*, he thought. *I wonder if I'll ever see her again.* He hadn't seen his mother for a couple of months at least; not since he'd been on the move with his brother, Tom. Their once safe lives were now a hectic blur of trying to stay one step ahead of the authorities. Tom's crime was serious. It was only a matter of time before the sheriff would figure it all out. Daniel was sick of it.

ELEMENTS OF LITERATURE

8   "Look, kid," Tom said. "Mother's not here. Maybe we'll be able to see her again one day. But right now, I'm all you've got."

9   "Great," Daniel said with disgust. "A liar *and* a thief. You promised no more stealing. You promised you'd get a job. But no. You had to go and steal again. And now they're after you."

10   The older brother took a canvas bag off a peg and said, "Put your things in here, Daniel. Now. We're leaving."

11   "No," said the boy.

12   "What do you mean, no? You saw those men. They're riding hard and they'll find this barn soon enough. I don't plan to be here when they do."

13   "Fine. You leave. I'm staying."

14   "You can't stay. Now, you can walk out those doors with me or I can carry you out. But you aren't staying."

15   "I'm staying. I'm not running anymore, Tom. I'm not the thief. You can run. But I'm staying."

16   "What do you think they'll do to you? Let you stay in this barn? Hah! They'll lock you up and then send you off to one of those orphanages. You want that? You want to be an orphan?" Tom said as he pulled Daniel up. "Now pack."

17   "No," said the boy. "I'm staying."

18   Tom threw the bag at his younger brother, expecting him to catch it. But Daniel wasn't prepared for the force of the throw and fell backward as the bag crashed into his stomach. He landed on the hay bale, knocking the lantern over. Instantly, the brothers smelled the smoke and saw licks of flame from the lantern quickly spread to the dry hay. Flames were leaping upward as smoke filled the barn.

19   "Run!" Tom shouted as he pulled Daniel to his feet.

20   They quickly ran outside to safety as fire spread across the old barn.

21   Then Tom looked across the field and saw men riding fast on horses. "We gotta run!" he screamed. He started running through the field, hoping to hide in the tall stalks of corn.

22   But Daniel didn't run. He stood alone, watching the barn burn. Tom looked once over his shoulder for Daniel, but he knew that his younger brother wouldn't follow.

The Barn

Directions: Before reading the MiniRead "The Barn," look at the following words taken from the story. Think about how these words could be connected, and write your Story Impression on the lines below. Make sure to keep the words in the same order as listed while writing your Story Impression. You may want to sketch your ideas first on the back of this sheet.

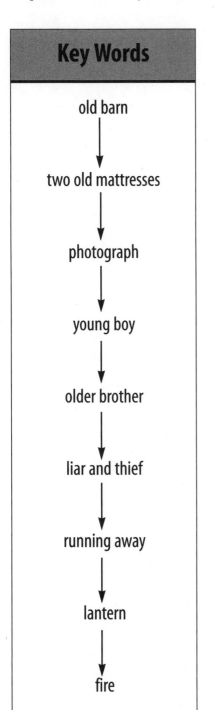

Key Words

old barn

↓

two old mattresses

↓

photograph

↓

young boy

↓

older brother

↓

liar and thief

↓

running away

↓

lantern

↓

fire

My Story Impression:

Three Skeleton Key

Directions: Before you read "Three Skeleton Key" (Pupil's Edition, page 64), look at the following key words related to the story. Think about how these words might be connected in a story. Then, on the lines below, write your Story Impression, predicting what you think the story will be about. Remember to keep the words in the same order they are listed. You may want to sketch your ideas first on the back of this page.

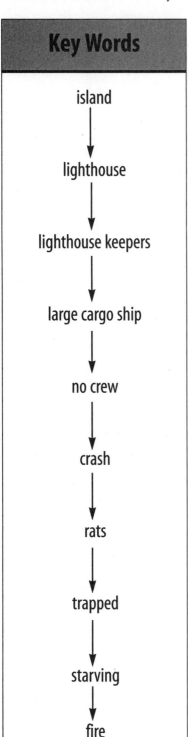

Key Words

island
↓
lighthouse
↓
lighthouse keepers
↓
large cargo ship
↓
no crew
↓
crash
↓
rats
↓
trapped
↓
starving
↓
fire

My Story Impression:

....
....
....
....
....
....
....
....
....
....
....
....
....
....
....
....
....

A Day's Wait

Directions: After you have read "A Day's Wait" (Pupil's Edition, page 80), complete the chart by answering the questions from the *Question* column. You may have several comments under the *It Says* and *I Say* columns for each question, but you should have only one answer under the *And So* column for each question. Continue your answers on the back of this sheet if necessary.

Question	It Says . . . + (What the text says)	I Say . . . = (My thoughts)	And So . . . (My inference)
1. How does Schatz deal with his illness? What inference can you make about the kind of person he is?			
2. The author never directly says that Papa loves his son. How do you know what the father feels for Schatz? What inference can you make about how people express love?			
3. Was Schatz afraid to die? What inference can you make about fear?			

A New Life

April 3, 1860

1   Today our ship sailed into New York. New York must be the most magnificent city in the world. It's bigger than the city of Cork—my home in Ireland. From the ship, we can see only buildings.

2   Every day, ships arrive with more and more people, mostly from Ireland and Germany. A man I met on the ship told me that someday there would be a million people living in New York. I don't think there are that many people in the world.

3   Our journey from Ireland to America has been long and scary. Sometimes on this trip I have wondered if it would have been better to stay in Ireland. My family has been living in a large area deep down in the ship. Hundreds of families were crowded together there. People were sick because the ship rolled up and down on the waves. Trash was everywhere. The rotting garbage smelled terrible.

4   Every night, my parents, brothers, sister, and I squeezed into a tiny space. Wharf rats ran across our cots. Our filthy, torn blankets were crawling with bedbugs. Every morning we were covered with bites. My worst nightmares were never this bad.

5   My sister, Caitlin, has been very sick. Black boils covered her arms and legs for awhile. She coughed up blood on her handkerchief. We sat up with her many nights, as she had the fever. She is better now, but many others with the same boils died.

6   We had little food on the trip. We ate only what we brought with us. My parents are thinner. I think they've been giving their share of the food to me and my brothers and sister. No two people have made as many sacrifices as my parents. They are the kindest, most giving people, and they deserve more than

A New Life *(cont'd)*

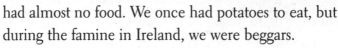

what they have had.

7   My family has been hungry longer than I have been alive. Nothing is worse than being hungry. The potatoes started rotting in the ground fifteen years ago. Since then, my family has had almost no food. We once had potatoes to eat, but during the famine in Ireland, we were beggars.

8   Yet, we are better off than some. Hundreds of people in our district in Ireland starved to death. Fever killed hundreds more. At times there were too many to bury, and the bodies had to be stacked in a back room.

9   My father says the famine was caused by a fungus. My mother says it is England's fault. Mother says the British took all of our food and left us nothing but potatoes. "When the potatoes died, we died," my mother said.

10   I don't know who is right. It doesn't matter. We are starting a new life now. Our lives here will be better and easier. We will spend a few more days on the ship to take care of some papers so that we can enter America. Then, we will move in with my uncle in Trenton. He has lived in America for five years. He says, "America is the greatest place in the world."

11   They say there are many opportunities in America. We have no money now, but we will work hard. We will save our money, and, someday, we will buy land of our own.

—Eamon O'Connor

Mini Read

A New Life

Part 1. Directions: After you read the MiniRead "A New Life," read each of the following statements. On the line provided, write *Fact* if the statement is a fact or *Opinion* if it is an opinion. In the space provided, explain your answer.

.... **1.** "Today our ship sailed into New York."

Explanation: ....

.... **2.** "New York must be the most magnificent city in the world."

Explanation: ....

.... **3.** "No two people have made as many sacrifices as my parents. They are the kindest, most giving people . . ."

Explanation: ....

.... **4.** "We once had potatoes to eat, but during the famine in Ireland, we were beggars."

Explanation: ....

Part 2. Directions: Read each of the following statements. On the line provided, write *Fact* if the statement is a fact and *Opinion* if the statement is an opinion. Then, reformulate fact statements into opinion statements and opinion statements into fact statements. You might need to add or delete some information to make your reformulation work.

.... **5.** "Nothing is worse than being hungry."

Reformulation: ....

....

.... **6.** "We had little food on the trip."

Reformulation: ....

....

.... **7.** "America is the greatest place in the world."

Reformulation: ....

....

.... **8.** "He has lived in America for five years."

Reformulation: ....

....

from Homesick

SKILL DISTINGUISHING FACT FROM OPINION | **STRATEGY** TEXT REFORMULATION

Part 1. Directions: After reading "Homesick" (Pupil's Edition, page 104), read each of the following statements taken from the selection. On the line provided, write *Fact* if the statement is a fact or *Opinion* if it is an opinion. In the space provided, explain your answer.

1. "And I was on the wrong side of the globe." (page 105)

Explanation: _____

2. "He grabbed my right arm and twisted it behind my back." (page 107)

Explanation: _____

3. "Now there was a girl, I thought, who was worth crying over." (page 110)

Explanation: _____

4. "Miss Williams was pinch-faced and bossy." (page 106)

Explanation: _____

5. "I never saw anyone give money to a beggar." (page 110)

Explanation: _____

6. "The grandest street in Hankow was the Bund, which ran along beside the Yangtze River." (page 111)

Explanation: _____

Part 2. Directions: Choose one fact statement and one opinion statement from Part 1. Then, reformulate the fact statement into an opinion statement and the opinion statement into a fact statement. You might need to add or delete some information to make your reformulation work.

Fact 7. _____

Reformulation: _____

Opinion 8. _____

Reformulation: _____

ELEMENTS OF LITERATURE

Active Reader's Practice Book | *25*

Take a Look at Yourself

1   "Hey," the voice hollered. "Hey! You! Look here at me." He waited a long time, then tried again. "You. You up there. Hey Too Tall Tim! Look here, down here." Nothing. Finally Jason sat down on the floor. He couldn't believe it. No one was listening. No one. Not even his brother Tim. What was wrong with all those giants? Just because they were big people, did they think they didn't have to listen to him?

2   Okay, so maybe he didn't always listen to people when he was big, but that was different. He didn't like being a mere two inches tall. Well, maybe he made a wish about being short enough to sneak under doorways so he could go wherever he wanted, but who would have ever thought that wish would come true? What a terrible time for his personal genie to decide to start granting his wishes. "Okay, okay," Jason thought to himself, "maybe I had been a little rude to that short kid in our class. Maybe calling him Mr. No Body was rude, but it sure made everyone laugh."

3   Jason looked around. He didn't like being two inches tall. Now who had no body? When Jason was his real size, he was always the tallest, the strongest in his class. And maybe, Jason remembered, he was also the rudest. Maybe he had too much fun making fun of others who weren't as tall and strong as he was.

4   Suddenly, the door opened and Jason's worst nightmare appeared—a cat. Jason didn't feel as brave as he had always felt; he suddenly felt afraid, something he had never felt before. He started doing something he hadn't done since preschool before: He started crying. "Oh Mr. Genie?" Jason said softly as the cat padded near him. "This would be a great time to grant another wish."

5   Jason had never liked cats in the first place. Now he liked them even less. Looking up at the striped fur of Buster, he felt as if he were looking at a tiger. Buster turned and his green eyes bored into Jason's. He lifted one white paw, claws reaching out, stretching the paw silently into the air toward Jason. The boy was about the size of a

mouse. This is it, Jason thought. This is what I get for being so stupid, so selfish, and so mean. This is what I get for wishing I could be small enough to sneak out at night. The cat's giant paw began to wave in the air like a magician's hand over a magic hat. Suddenly Jason heard a loud pop, and a cloud of smoke formed. When the smoke cleared, there was the genie.

6   "So, what's the problem?" the genie said to Jason, his chewing gum popping.

7   "You're about to get me killed. That's what's the problem," Jason replied, his voice shaking.

8   "Hey, it's not my fault you wished the wrong wish. I'm just here to grant wishes. It's not my job to decide which wishes are dumb ones. Want some gum?"

9   "No, I don't want any gum! I want my old size back. I don't care about sneaking out anymore. Just make me tall."

10   "That sounds pretty funny coming from a guy who used to spend all his time making up ugly names to call people," said the genie.

11   "Okay, okay, I wasn't such a nice guy. I just wanted everyone to laugh and to like me. I didn't even think about what I was doing, but I guess it was pretty bad. I guess I shouldn't be lying and sneaking around at night, either."

12   "You guess?"

13   "No, I really mean it."

14   The genie stopped chewing for a moment. His old knees cracked as he sat on the floor so he could get closer to the boy. He studied Jason's eyes carefully to see if he was telling the truth. This time there was no loud pop, just silence as the smoke rose. When it cleared, Jason was sitting on the bed, stroking Buster, who was stretched out happily in his lap.

Mini Read

Take a Look at Yourself

SKILL RECOGNIZING COMPARISON AND CONTRAST | **STRATEGY** SEMANTIC DIFFERENTIAL SCALES

Directions: Read the first page of the MiniRead "Take a Look at Yourself." Place a **1** in the circle that best describes Jason at the beginning of the story. Then, read the second page. Put a **2** in the circle that best describes him at the end of the story. Be sure to give reasons for each rating.

Jason

1. Friendly   Hostile

◯ ◯ ◯ ◯ ◯

Explanation for 1 _____

Explanation for 2 _____

2. Thoughtful   Thoughtless

◯ ◯ ◯ ◯ ◯

Explanation for 1 _____

Explanation for 2 _____

3. Fearful   Fearless

◯ ◯ ◯ ◯ ◯

Explanation for 1 _____

Explanation for 2 _____

4. Honest   Dishonest

◯ ◯ ◯ ◯ ◯

Explanation for 1 _____

Explanation for 2 _____

from Barrio Boy

SKILL RECOGNIZING COMPARISON AND CONTRAST | **STRATEGY** SEMANTIC DIFFERENTIAL SCALES

Directions: After reading "Barrio Boy" (Pupil's Edition, page 125), think about how Ernesto changes during the story. Mark a **1** in the circle that would best describe Ernesto when he entered first grade. Mark a **2** in the circle that best describes Ernesto at the end of the story. Be sure to explain your ratings.

Ernesto

1. Embarrassed   ○ ○ ○ ○ ○   **Proud**

Explanation for **1** ....

Explanation for **2** ....

2. Confident   ○ ○ ○ ○ ○   **Timid**

Explanation for **1** ....

Explanation for **2** ....

3. Lucky   ○ ○ ○ ○ ○   **Unlucky**

Explanation for **1** ....

Explanation for **2** ....

4. Brave   ○ ○ ○ ○ ○   **Fearful**

Explanation for **1** ....

Explanation for **2** ....

5. Successful   ○ ○ ○ ○ ○   **Unsuccessful**

Explanation for **1** ....

Explanation for **2** ....

6. Happy   ○ ○ ○ ○ ○   **Unhappy**

Explanation for **1** ....

Explanation for **2** ....

Word Up—or Down?

1 Words are everywhere. If you stop reading this and look around the room, you'll probably see words. Drive down a street, and you will see lots of words. If you go to a convenience store, visit a department store, or stop by a video-rental store, at all three you'll see words! There are long words like *microscopic* (which actually means "extremely small") and short words like *ton* (which actually means "a huge amount"). While you look at the words that are all around you, notice how funny and confusing they can be.

2 Some words seem to mean the opposite of what they say. For instance, think about the word *driveway*. It sounds like a place to drive, but no! A driveway is a place to park. And a *parkway* isn't a place to park but instead is a place to drive! *Apartment* has the word *apart* in it, but it means a building in which individual homes are together.

3 The confusion continues. Why can people give up but never give down? Why do teachers always tell you to hurry up and never to hurry down? Why can a building burn up while it is also burning down? Why is it important to call someone by his or her name but also important not to be a name-caller? Why do friends hang out instead of hang in? Why is it nice to be called cool but awful to be called cold? If an employer is the person who hires someone and an employee is the one who does the work, then why doesn't *worker* mean the same thing as *employer* and *workee* the same thing as *employee*?

4 Spellings can also change the meanings of words. Have you ever noticed how just one let-ter can completely

change a word? For instance, *hop* is just *hop* until you add an *e*, and then you get *hope*. *Fat* is just *fat* until you add an *e*, and then you have *fate*. *He* is *he* until you add *t*, and then you have *the*. Of course, if you add an *s* instead, the *he* is *she*. Confused? Well, start with one of the two simplest words of all: *I*. Add the letter *t* and now you have *it*. Put an *s* at the beginning and you've turned *it* into *sit*. *Sit* is a good word, nothing strange about it, but add the letter *p* and now you have *spit*. If you don't want *spit*, then change that *i* to an *o* and now you've got *spot*. If *spot* isn't the word you were after, change the *p* to an *h* and now you've got *shot*. Drop the *s* really fast and you're down to *hot*. Change the *o* to an *a*, and see the word *hat*. Say goodbye to the *h* and hello to *at*. Send the *t* away fast and you are left with another of the simplest words of them all: *a*.

5 From the simplest words to the most complex, some words direct us; some inform us; some even delight and entertain us. But many of them seem to exist simply to confuse us!

Word Up—or Down?

SKILL DETERMINING THE MAIN IDEA | **STRATEGY** MOST IMPORTANT WORD

Part 1. Directions: After reading the MiniRead "Word Up—or Down?" look back through it and choose what you consider the most important word in the text. Then, complete the following statements on the lines provided.

1. The most important word in the MiniRead is ....

2. List several reasons for choosing this word. Be sure that your reasons are supported with examples directly from the MiniRead.
I chose this word because ....

....

....

....

3. Using the most important word I chose, I now think that the main idea of this MiniRead is

....

....

Part 2. Directions: Fill in the drawing of a hand below. Write the main idea in the palm of the hand. Then, on each finger write down one supporting detail. A supporting detail is a fact or idea from the MiniRead that supports or explains the main idea.

Names/Nombres

SKILL DETERMINING THE MAIN IDEA | **STRATEGY** MOST IMPORTANT WORD

Part 1. Directions: After reading "Names/Nombres" (Pupil's Edition, page 145), look back through the selection and choose what you consider to be the most important word in this story. Then, complete the following statements on the lines provided.

1. The most important word in this story is ....

2. List several reasons for choosing this word. Be sure that your reasons are supported with examples directly from the selection.
   I chose this word because

   ....

   ....

   ....

   ....

   ....

   ....

3. Using the most important word I chose, I now think that the main idea of this selection is

   ....

   ....

Part 2. Directions:

In small groups, listen to and share the most important words selected by group members. Think about the reasons group members give for their choices, especially for word choices different from your own. What do you think of their words and their reasons for choosing those words? After you have finished your discussions with group members, complete the following statements.

4. After my group's discussion, I chose .... as my most important word.

5. I changed/didn't change my mind because ....

   ....

   ....

6. After group discussion, I now believe that the main idea of this selection is ....

   ....

The Naming of Names

Part 1. Directions: Decide with a partner whether you will read the "The Naming of Names" (Pupil's Edition, page 152) silently or aloud. As you read, stop about every three or four paragraphs and take turns saying something about what you just read, including any comments you can make about monitoring your comprehension. In the chart below, write a check mark in the appropriate column for each type of comment you make.

Prediction	Comment	Question	Connection

Part 2. Directions: Think about the Say Something dialogue you had with your partner, and answer the following questions on the lines provided. You can continue your answers on the back of this page or on a separate sheet of paper.

1. If someone had been listening in on your Say Something dialogue, what would they have heard? Give a summary. ....

....

2. Did you answer any questions for your partner? Did your partner answer any questions for you? What were the questions? What questions remain unanswered? ....

....

3. Looking at your chart above, what type of comment did you make the most? Why do you think you made that type the most? ....

....

4. Think about the statements you made about monitoring your comprehension. How did the Say Something strategy help you? ....

....

5. If you do a Say Something again, how will you do it differently? ....

....

The Princess and the Amphibian

1   Once upon a time there was an <u>egotistical</u> princess. She was just the opposite of her sister, who was thoughtful and humble. The princess had thick, long, dark hair. Her eyes were like shiny, black <u>obsidian</u> from a volcano. Her arms were <u>Herculean</u> from working out. She looked good, and she knew it.

2   The princess would have been happy except for one <u>appalling</u> thing: She had promised to marry an <u>amphibian</u>— namely, an ugly, bulgy-eyed frog. She was only five years old when she made the promise. She had gotten in trouble for being mean to another kid and had made this promise to convince her parents she really could be nice. How could she be held <u>accountable</u> for something she had said when she was so <u>callow</u>? Wasn't there a <u>legal precedent</u> or law that applied when this happened to someone else? Couldn't she get out of this? Why couldn't her sister marry the green croaker? Why did she always have to be the one in trouble? Why did she always wind up promising to do things to pay for her <u>infractions</u>?

3   Her father, the king, felt sorry for her, but he also felt she needed to learn a lesson. "A promise is a promise. You need to learn to live up to your pledge. You <u>assured</u> us you would marry Mr. Green," he kept saying. Mr. Green was the bulgy-eyed pond hopper's name—very original.

4   "He couldn't even come up with a good name," the princess thought to herself. Her mother, the queen, privately thought the frog was better than the princess' last <u>suitor</u>, Carl. Carl was <u>obnoxious</u>; Mr. Green, however, was thoughtful and sweet.

5   The princess tried to <u>contrive a scheme</u>, make a plan, plot an escape, but nothing worked out. "I wonder if the royal chef knows how to cook frogs' legs?" she said to herself. Meanwhile,

her <u>earnest</u> sister worked hard to help the princess. She talked to her <u>incessantly</u>, day and night, trying to convince her that this would all work out. She offered to marry the frog herself, but the king and queen wouldn't hear of it. "A promise is a promise," they kept <u>reiterating</u>.

6   The wedding day arrived. The princess woke up when the sun was just peeking over the horizon. She clamped the pillow over her head and refused to get out of bed. So everything for the wedding ceremony was brought into the bedroom: chairs for guests, flowers, cake, punch, and the minister. She peeked out from under the pillow. Standing in very close <u>proximity</u> was you-know-who, using his tongue to catch flies that had flown in the open window. The princess moaned and screamed, "This is the worst nightmare I've ever had! If I ever get out of this I'll never be so egotistical and mean again as long as I live."

7   Suddenly, she woke up, the last sentence of her dream <u>reverberating</u> in her mind. She peeked out from under the covers and breathed a long sigh. It had been a dream.

8   Her eyes focused on the light faintly <u>radiating</u> from the window. There on the windowsill sat a huge, ugly amphibian.

9   Has the princess changed because her dream taught her an important lesson? Is she nice, sweet, and ready to give everyone a chance? Will she now be more like her sister?

10   She picks up a running shoe, one from her favorite pair with the blue stripes, and flings it as hard as she can at the window. The shoe misses the frog and crashes through the glass. She's in trouble again.

The Princess and the Amphibian

A

SKILL USING CONTEXT CLUES | **STRATEGY** VOCABULARY DEVELOPMENT: CONTEXT CLUES

Directions: Study and learn the following types of context clues.

1. Definition/Explanation Clues

Sometimes authors actually **define** a word or explain it in the same sentence in which the word appears.

Example: *A symbol is something that stands for something else.*

In this sentence, the word *symbol* is directly defined.

2. Restatement/Synonym Clues

Sometimes writers **restate** difficult words with easier ones. They are using **synonyms** as the context clue.

Example: *The boy used a goad, a long stick, to direct the elephant's movements.*

In this sentence, *goad* is restated as a more common term, *long stick.*

Example: *The food was so bland that everyone called it tasteless.*

In this sentence the word *bland* is understood once you reach the word *tasteless.*

3. Contrast/Antonym Clues

While a restatement clue repeats the meaning of the unknown word by using a synonym, a **contrast clue** explains the meaning by providing you with an **antonym** of the unknown word.

Example: *Some horses are docile, but others are very excitable and hard to manage.*

The word *docile* is explained through antonyms rather than synonyms. The signal word *but* (see box above) lets you know that the opposite of whatever was just stated is about to appear. In the above sentence you realize that *docile* must mean the opposite of *very excitable* and *hard to manage.*

4. Inference/General Context Clues

Inference or **general context clues** aren't as obvious as other types of clues. The writer expects you to infer the meaning of the unfamiliar word by thinking about the relationship between the word and other information in the text. These clues may even be a few sentences away from the unfamiliar word.

Example: *I am alone, unseen, and imperceptible to all. No one says "hi" or asks me to join them for lunch.*

You can figure out what the word *imperceptible* means by thinking about the words *alone* and *unseen* and about how you would feel if others acted like they never saw you or never acknowledged your existence. You have inferred the meaning by using words in the sentence and your own knowledge.

Common Signal Words

Signal words are often found with restatement/synonym and contrast/antonym clues. They tell you that an explanation or an opposite meaning is coming up. Here are some frequently used signal words:

Restatement/Synonym

for example	especially
these	like
such as	so . . . that

Contrast/Antonym

on the other hand	although
still	however
but	by contrast
not	while

The Princess and the Amphibian   B
SKILL USING CONTEXT CLUES | STRATEGY VOCABULARY DEVELOPMENT: CONTEXT CLUES

Directions: After reading the MiniRead "The Princess and the Amphibian," identify the context clues for the underlined words in the sentences below, and write them on the lines provided. Then, explain what you think each word means, basing your explanation on the context clue.

> **Example:**
>
> The extraordinary pianist was a <u>prodigy</u>; her talent was apparent when she was only five years old.
>
> **Context Clue:** *extraordinary, talent, five years old*
>
> **Type of Context Clue:** *inference/general context*
>
> **Explanation:** *The pianist is talented, and she has been able to play well from a very young age. A prodigy must be an especially gifted young person.*

1. callow   Even though Elaine was the oldest, she was more <u>callow</u> than her younger but more sophisticated and mature sisters.

Context Clue(s): ....

Explanation: ....

2. infraction   Wearing hats to school was an <u>infraction</u> against the school's dress code. Because of this, all students were discouraged from violating the dress code by leaving their hats at home.

Context Clue(s): ....

Explanation: ....

3. obnoxious   The home team fans became <u>obnoxious</u> during the last quarter when they began to throw trash and shout insults at the visiting team fans in the stands.

Context Clue(s): ....

Explanation: ....

4. reiterating   "Why do you keep <u>reiterating</u> what you have already stated?" Carla asked Mike as he practiced his presentation. "There's no need to repeat what you've said before."

Context Clue(s): ....

Explanation: ....

5. proximity   The firefighter, seeing the close <u>proximity</u> of the curtains to the stove, knew right away how the fire started.

Context Clue(s): ....

Explanation: ....

After Twenty Years

SKILL USING CONTEXT CLUES | **STRATEGY** VOCABULARY DEVELOPMENT: CONTEXT CLUES

Directions: Read each of the sentences below. Then, write down and explain what clues, if any, the author gives you to the meaning of the word. The author may give you one of the following clues:

Defining the word within the sentence (Definition/Explanation Clue)

Restating the word with an easier one (Restatement/Synonym Clue)

Putting a word that means the opposite in the sentence (Contrast/Antonym Clue)

Giving information that you can use to infer the word's meaning (Inference/General Context Clue)

Example: He felt so much <u>remorse</u> for what he had done that he confessed to the crime.

Context Clue: *Inference/General Context Clue. You can tell that he felt bad about what he had done or he wouldn't have confessed. Remorse must mean "feeling guilty."*

Write down the context clues to the underlined words in the sentences below.

1. intricate

He had planned a long time for his escape, and with every movement he kept in mind his <u>intricate</u> and detailed plan.

Context Clue(s): ....

....

2. dismal

The sky was gray and <u>dismal</u> compared to the warm light inside the tent.

Context Clue(s): ....

....

3. egotism

His <u>egotism</u> made him believe he could escape when no one else had ever been able to. However, no matter how grand his plan might be, he would not succeed.

Context Clue(s): ....

....

4. simultaneously

When two people look at one another <u>simultaneously</u>, they turn and look at each other at exactly the same time.

Context Clue(s): ....

....

A Mason-Dixon Memory

SKILL MAKING PREDICTIONS | **STRATEGY** STORY IMPRESSIONS

Part 1. Directions: Before reading "A Mason-Dixon Memory" (Pupil's Edition, page 205), look at the list of key words and phrases related to the selection and brainstorm how these words might be related in the story. Write down your Story Impression predicting what you think the story will be about, using these words and phrases. Keep the words in the same order they are listed. Continue writing on the back of this sheet if necessary.

My Story Impression:

Key Words
1991
↓
high school golf tournament
↓
African American player
↓
whites only
↓
memories from 1959
↓
trip to Washington, D.C.
↓
amusement park

....

....

....

....

....

....

....

....

....

....

Part 2. Directions: After reading "A Mason-Dixon Memory," review your Story Impression. How close was your prediction to the actual story? On the lines below, explain the ways in which your story was similar to or different from the selection.

....

....

....

....

....

What Are You Saying?

Liliana

1   Liliana thought Elvis Presley was king. His music rocked, and she could hear the beat even if her father's old turntable wasn't moving. The one thing Liliana and her father saw eye to eye on was the fact that they'd both sit and listen to Elvis till the cows came home.

2   That's why her father always told her the story of how he saw Elvis in concert on a night that turned out to be a real frog strangler. It was the first time he had asked her mother out on a date, and he was glad he had fixed the leak in his car roof. His car was a rattletrap, but he had it all shined up, spiffy, and ready to roll. He picked up Louise on time and began the drive to the concert. On the way the sky opened up and poured such a gully washer that they had to pull off to the side of the road. While they waited for the storm to blow over, they talked about their lives, what they wanted to do when they graduated, and how they felt about all kinds of things. Liliana's father always said that if that storm hadn't come up, things might have been different. Just sitting in that gas guzzler listening to the rain pound on the roof made for a nice situation to just jaw awhile and get to know each other.

Kathleen

3   Kathleen had lived in New York City all her life. Her friend, Joan, was from San Antonio. They were good friends and visited each other often. They had only one problem. Sometimes they didn't understand each other.

4   For example, one day as they were leaving Kathleen's New York apartment on Eighty-fifth Street,

What Are You Saying? *(cont'd)*

Kathleen turned to Joan and said, "Hand me my pocketbook." Joan handed her the paperback book she was reading. Another time when they were eating lunch, Joan asked for some hot sauce. Instead of salsa, Kathleen gave her a skinny little bottle stuffed with a bunch of tiny peppers in a clear liquid.

5   When Kathleen visited Joan in San Antonio, she tried to use her Spanish. When she was asking directions she kept saying "donday" all the time. People stared and Joan told her to be quiet. In a store, a salesclerk overheard Kathleen talking to Joan and said, "You're not from around here, are you?"

6   "No, I'm visiting from New York," said Kathleen.

7   "Well, y'ought to come down here more often," said the salesclerk. "Y'all come back soon, now."

8   Kathleen turned to Joan and said, "Why does she keep talking about a boat? There's no lake around here."

Richard

9   Richard was visiting Liz in England. She was an artist and lived in a loft in London. After supper one night, Liz asked Richard if he would wash up. Later, she got mad because the dishes were still dirty. He had washed his hands.

10   The next day Richard decided to go out and explore London on his own. Liz said, "Be sure to ring me up." Richard was confused by Liz's request—was she talking about a bell or a ring? When he came back that afternoon, Liz seemed upset.

11   "Why didn't you ring me up? I was waiting for your call," she said. Richard looked puzzled for a second, and then said, "Oh, sorry, I forgot."

queue ('kyü)

12   "Well, we'd better leave now for the film, or the queue will be quite long. I think we have time to take the tube instead of a cab," said Liz.

13   Without pausing to ask Liz what a queue or a tube was, Richard followed Liz out to the street. Liz quickly walked to a set of stairs going down into the ground; a sign labeled "Underground" marked the stairs' entrance. Once Richard saw where Liz was headed, he smiled and asked her, "Why didn't you say we were taking the subway?"

14   "What's a subway?" Liz asked with a puzzled look on her face.

ELEMENTS OF LITERATURE

MiniRead

What Are You Saying?

SKILL UNDERSTANDING REGIONAL AND CULTURAL SAYINGS | **STRATEGY** THINK-ALOUD

Directions: Work with a partner to read the MiniRead "What Are You Saying?" and make Think-Aloud comments. One partner should read aloud the second section, pausing to make comments, while the other partner uses a tally mark to identify those comments in the *Tally* column below. Then, switch roles and continue to the end of the MiniRead.

Think-Aloud Tally Sheet

Listener:_____

Think-Aloud Comments	Tally
Predicting what happens next	
Picturing the text	
Making comparisons	
Identifying problems	
Fixing problems	
Making comments	

The No-Guitar Blues

Skill Understanding Regional and Cultural Sayings | **Strategy** Think-Aloud

Directions: Work with a partner to read "The No-Guitar Blues" (Pupil's Edition, page 217) and make Think-Aloud comments. One partner should read aloud the second section, pausing to make comments, while the other partner uses a tally mark to identify those comments in the *Tally* column below. Then, switch roles and continue to the end of the selection.

Think-Aloud Tally Sheet

Listener:_____

Think-Aloud Comments	Tally
Predicting what happens next	
Picturing the text	
Making comparisons	
Identifying problems	
Fixing problems	
Making comments	

ELEMENTS OF LITERATURE

Bargain

Part 1. Directions: After reading "Bargain" (Pupil's Edition, page 230), read the following questions and conclusions *(And So)* and then find information in the text that supports those conclusions. Record that information under the *It Says* column. In the *I Say* column, write your thoughts about the *It Says* statements. Then, check to see if the information in the *It Says* and *I Say* columns supports the conclusions given in the *And So* column. Continue your answers on the back of this sheet if necessary.

Question	And So (Conclusion)	It Says . . . = (What the text says)	I Say . . . (My thoughts)
1. What kind of person is Slade?	Slade is a bully who is not very smart and is prejudiced against certain people. He thinks violence is a way to get whatever you want.		
2. What kind of person is Mr. Baumer?	Mr. Baumer is determined. He is smart. He is willing to be patient until he can get what he wants the way he wants it.		
3. Who or what caused Slade's death?	Mr. Baumer caused Slade's death.		

Part 2. Directions: Answer the following questions on the back of this sheet.

Do you disagree with any of the conclusions listed above? If yes, which one(s)? What conclusion would you have drawn instead? Why?

ELEMENTS OF LITERATURE

Amigo Brothers

SKILL RECOGNIZING COMPARISON AND CONTRAST | **STRATEGY** LIKERT SCALES

Directions: After reading "Amigo Brothers" (Pupil's Edition, page 245), respond to each of the following items by circling *Strongly Agree, Agree, Disagree,* or *Strongly Disagree.* Then, in the space provided, write a brief explanation of your choice.

1. Antonio and Felix both want to win the fight.

Strongly Agree	Agree	Disagree	Strongly Disagree

Explanation: ....

....

....

....

2. Felix is more worried than Antonio about fighting a friend.

Strongly Agree	Agree	Disagree	Strongly Disagree

Explanation: ....

....

....

....

3. Antonio is a better fighter than Felix.

Strongly Agree	Agree	Disagree	Strongly Disagree

Explanation: ....

....

....

....

Success Story

Fade in:

Exterior — Suburban Driveway — Day

Two young boys play basketball in the driveway of a suburban house. Richie, 11, struggles to guard his older brother, Steve, who is almost a foot taller. Richie is wearing a Boston Celtics jersey with the number five on it. Steve wears a Los Angeles Lakers jersey with the number fifteen on it.

> **RICHIE** (*voice over*): My brother and I were always competing. In school. In sports. In life.

Steve fakes to his left, and Richie goes for it. Steve spins around and heads in the opposite direction. Richie tries to change directions, but loses his balance.

> **RICHIE** (*voice over*): Steve usually won.

On his way to the hoop, Steve brushes past Richie, who goes sprawling onto the pavement. Steve makes an easy layup, and Richie jumps up, picks up the basketball, and starts yelling at Steve.

> **RICHIE** (*voice over*): And when we weren't competing, we were having arguments.

Steve snaps back once and grabs the ball away from Richie.

> **RICHIE** (*voice over*): Steve usually won those, too.

Steve starts showing Richie the move he just made, only this time in slow motion. Richie watches closely as Steve walks through the move.

> **RICHIE** (*voice over*): But no matter how many times he beat me, he never rubbed it in or acted all high and mighty. Instead, he would try to teach me something.

Steve wraps up his instruction, and he and Richie start playing for real again. Steve dribbles the ball, then fakes left. This time, Richie doesn't budge.

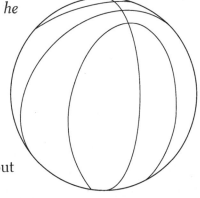

> **RICHIE** (*voice over*): I can still hear him. "Richie," he would say, "losing is nothing but

an opportunity to learn and get better."
Steve fakes again; Richie stands firm.

Cut to:

Interior—Basketball Floor—Night

The arena is packed with cheering fans. On the floor, a player for the Los Angeles Lakers takes a pass and turns to face the defender, an intense young man with the number five on his Boston Celtics jersey.

RICHIE *(voice over)*: Steve was always a better basketball player than me, but I was the one who made it to the pros.

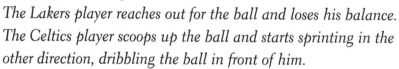

The Lakers player fakes to his left, then tries to drive right. But the Celtics player doesn't take the fake, and covers the Lakers player tightly.

RICHIE *(voice over)*: Steve should have made it, too.

The Lakers player tries to change directions, but the Celtics player reaches and slaps the ball away.

RICHIE *(voice over)*: He was good enough.

The Lakers player reaches out for the ball and loses his balance. The Celtics player scoops up the ball and starts sprinting in the other direction, dribbling the ball in front of him.

RICHIE *(voice over)*: And he wanted it as much as I did.

Boston's number five dribbles the ball down court. Several players chase after him, but he is too fast and has had too much of a head start.

RICHIE *(voice over)*: But when it came right down to it, there was one thing Steve wanted even more than to play in the NBA.

Boston's number five dunks the ball. The crowd roars.

Cut to:

Interior—Arena Box Seat—Night

A young man springs to his feet and pumps his fist in the air. He is beaming with pride.

RICHIE *(voice over)*: He wanted his little brother to make it.

MiniRead

Success Story

Part 1. Directions: Choose one part or the rest of the MiniRead "Success Story" to reformulate as a newspaper article or poem. Before writing your reformulation, answer the following questions:

1. Why did you choose this part of the MiniRead? ....

....

....

2. What information from this part of the MiniRead do you want to include in your reformulation?

....

....

....

3. Which type of text structure will you use for the reformulation—newspaper article or poem?

....

4. Why are you choosing that text structure? ....

....

Part 2. Directions: Begin writing your reformulation of the MiniRead. Continue writing on the back of this sheet or on your own paper, if necessary.

....

....

....

....

....

....

....

Brian's Song

Directions: Choose one of the following characters from "Brian's Song" (Pupil's Edition, page 274), and write by each letter a significant event or attitude that applies to that character, or to the teleplay as a whole. The first letter has been completed for you.

B   *is for Brian's best friend, who stuck by him.*

R   ....

I   ....

A   ....

N   ....

P   ....

I   ....

C   ....

C   ....

O   ....

L   ....

O   ....

G   ....

A   ....

L   ....

E   ....

S   ....

A   ....

Y   ....

E   ....

R   ....

S   ....

Project Salamander

1   It all made so much sense at the time. You see, the company needed to squeeze an extra crop into each growing season. That meant we had to plant the first crop earlier in the spring and harvest the last crop later in autumn. That also meant that we were running some risks. A late spring cold snap or an early fall freeze could wipe out a whole crop.

2   But the company scientists told us that we wouldn't lose more than two crops in the next five years. That was a risk we could live with.

3   Unfortunately, that's not how it worked out. For three years in a row, we had at least one crop failure. You don't have to be a genius to figure out what that could mean to the company. They weren't very happy, and neither were we.

4   That's where Project Salamander came in. What do salamanders have to do with corn? A lot more than I ever thought, that's for sure!

5   I'm still not sure how all of this works, but here's what the scientists told me. They said there is some kind of protein in salamander eggs that keeps them alive in frozen water. Don't ask me how, but you can put these proteins into corn seed and—bam!—you've got corn that won't freeze.

6   It was perfect. Our problem was solved. This new Supercorn could survive a cold snap, so we could plant an extra crop and not worry about the weather.

7   Of course, we went through all kinds of tests to make sure that the crop was safe, and everything checked out. So we planted a few test crops, and it seemed that each crop was better than the one before.

8   Everything was going great.

9   Then, early one morning, one of the workers noticed a bug on one of the plants. It looked like a ladybug, only much bigger and . . . well . . . uglier. The worker scooped the bug into a jar and took it to the lab. Our scientists took a look at it. They said they weren't too worried. After all, it was just one bug.

10   The next morning, another worker found a whole row of corn covered with bugs. Suddenly, everybody got nervous. All of the test fields were checked, and almost half of the corn had bugs. By evening, the bugs had spread throughout the entire test field. You could hardly hear yourself think over the awful sound of the bugs chewing.

11   That's not the worst news. We couldn't stop the bugs from spreading. They started showing up in all the fields, and before it was over the company didn't have a single ear of corn to its name.

12   We were all shocked, of course. It all happened so fast. One minute, everything is going fine. The next minute—bam!—you're out of the corn business.

13   It took awhile for our scientists to figure out what happened. Now, this is all way over my head, but I'll try to explain it as best I can. The scientists said that some kind of ordinary, normal bug got into one of the test fields and started chowing down on the corn.

14   Now this part even the scientists aren't quite sure about, but somehow our Supercorn turned those ordinary bugs into *Superbugs.* The chemicals we used to kill them were useless, and the Superbugs ate our whole crop.

15   So Project Salamander was a complete failure. But things are looking up. Our scientists have taken a protein from an elephant and put it into a beet. They tell me that the early results are very promising.

Project Salamander

SKILL RECOGNIZING CAUSES AND EFFECTS | **STRATEGY** TEXT REFORMULATION

Part 1: Directions: Write your reformulation of the MiniRead "Project Salamander" using the *If/Then* pattern on the lines provided. Continue writing on the back of this sheet if necessary.

Example: *If the company wants to get an extra crop each season, then we have to plant earlier in the spring and later in the fall.*

If ....

....

Then ....

....

If ....

....

Then ....

....

If ....

....

Then ....

Part 2: Directions: After writing your reformulation, answer the following questions on the lines provided.

1. What kinds of information did you include in your reformulation?

....

....

2. What kinds of information did you leave out of your reformulation?

....

....

3. How did reformulating the MiniRead into this pattern help you figure out the actions and results that occurred in the MiniRead?

....

User Friendly

SKILL RECOGNIZING CAUSES AND EFFECTS | **STRATEGY** TEXT REFORMULATION

Directions: After reading "User Friendly" (Pupil's Edition, page 357), use the lines below to write a Text Reformulation that shows cause-and-effect relationships throughout the selection. You will use the *If/Then* pattern to show causes and effects. The first pair of *If/Then* statements has been provided for you. Continue writing your reformulation on the back of this sheet if necessary.

If

Then

If

Then

If

Then

If

Then

Kevin turns on the computer in the morning,

it says, "Good morning, Kevin," gives basic information about the day, and asks him if he wants a printout.

Miss Awful

Directions: After reading "Miss Awful" (Pupil's Edition, page 368), respond to each of the following items by looking at the scale provided and marking an X in the circle that best represents the rating you would assign to Miss Orville for each quality listed. Then, explain why you gave Miss Orville the rating.

1. Miss Orville is a

good teacher ○　　　○　　　○　　　○　　　○ bad teacher

Explanation: ....

....

....

2. Miss Orville is

fair ○　　　○　　　○　　　○　　　○ unfair

Explanation: ....

....

....

3. Miss Orville is a

better teacher
than Miss Wilson ○　　　○　　　○　　　○　　　○ worse teacher
than Miss Wilson

Explanation: ....

....

....

ELEMENTS OF LITERATURE

Cos Gives It Up

1   What does Bill Cosby have in common with Robin Williams and Jim Carrey—besides being funny? Cosby's 1996 and 1997 combined income was thirty-six million dollars, an amount of money that placed him on *Forbes Magazine*'s 1997 Top 40 list of the wealthiest entertainers. He's there alongside other famous comics like Robin Williams and Jim Carrey. Although Cos doesn't shoot hoops, model clothes, or direct blockbuster movies for a living, he's definitely making big bucks from joking on the screen and stage. But Bill Cosby doesn't let the buck stop at the punch line.

2   Jokes aside, Cos is serious when it comes to money. Cosby has played many roles in television shows, movies, and his stand-up comedy routines, but he equally enjoys the role of giver and helper. As a benefactor, Cosby gives out of his own pocket to those who need it. Like other celebrities who make charitable donations, such as Oprah Winfrey, Steven Spielberg, and Michael Jordan, he can put his money where his mouth is when it comes to sharing his success with others. Frequently, Cosby does his stand-up routines or gives speeches for benefit performances that raise funds for deserving causes. He has donated twenty million dollars to Spelman College to build a variety of new facilities and pay for teaching positions. Before this, no individual had ever donated such a large amount to an African American college; only three other individual donations to any cause had been larger than his. Cosby and his wife, Camille, have also set up a foundation to support people with dyslexia (dis·lek'·sē·ə), a type of learning disability. The Future Filmmakers Program at New York University was established by Cosby to help encourage and provide opportunities for students in the film industry.

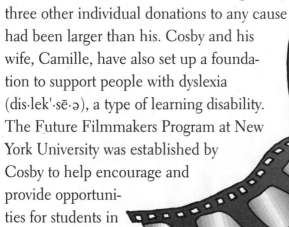

3   But Bill Cosby doesn't donate for recognition or fame; his acts of charity come from his heart and from his belief that the road to success starts with one important word—Education. This belief could seem kind of funny coming from someone who was a problem student in grade school, somebody who was better at cracking up his friends in class than cracking open a book. Cosby was determined to achieve his goals, despite his beginning struggles in school. Because he was a natural comedian but not a natural student, his road to success was not straight and immediate. At one point, he even dropped out of high school. Nicknamed Shorty because he was tall as a kid, Shorty did not come up short; he realized that he would never really succeed in a personal way if he didn't have some solid ground under him, and that ground was education. While working in the entertainment industry, he worked on his degrees. He became so focused on his goal that he eventually earned a Ph.D. in education—no joke. Although it may seem that Cosby's dream was to be in the spotlight, his personal dream was to finish college. You could say that education is no laughing matter to Bill Cosby, and donating his income to educational causes shows how serious he is.

4   If you ask anybody who Bill Cosby is, chances are good you'll get answers like, "comedian," "that actor who had his own sitcom," or even "that guy who does those funny pudding and gelatin commercials." Now you can add the role of benefactor to that list.

Cos Gives It Up

SKILL ESTABLISHING AND ADJUSTING PURPOSES FOR READING | **STRATEGY** SAVE THE LAST WORD FOR ME

Part 1. Directions: After reading the MiniRead "Cos Gives It Up," choose your favorite passage and copy it onto the lines provided.

"

....

....

....

....

....

....

....

....

"

....

Part 2. Directions: On the lines provided, answer the following questions.

1. Why did you choose this passage? ....

....

....

2. What were your purposes for reading the MiniRead? ....

....

....

3. In what ways did your purposes for reading change as you read "Cos Gives It Up"? Provide

examples from the MiniRead to support your answer. ....

....

....

The Only Girl in the World for Me

SKILL ESTABLISHING AND ADJUSTING PURPOSES FOR READING | **STRATEGY** SAVE THE LAST WORD FOR ME

Part 1. Directions: After reading "The Only Girl in the World for Me" (Pupil's Edition, page 387), choose your favorite passage and copy it on the lines provided.

"

....

....

....

....

....

....

....

....

....

....

....

....

....

....

"

....

Part 2. Directions: After you have copied the passage onto the lines above, use the back of this sheet to answer the following questions.

1. Why did you choose this passage as your favorite?

2. What do you think this passage means?

3. How did reading this passage change your purpose for reading the rest of this selection? In other words, did reading this passage make you want to read more or make you think other parts of the text might be funny? Did the passage remind you of yourself or a friend and make you want to read on to see if other parts did the same thing?

4. Why is it important to set a purpose for whatever you read? Is it just as important to be able to change that purpose?

ELEMENTS OF LITERATURE

Sky Woman

SKILL RECALLING WITH CHRONOLOGY | **STRATEGY** RETELLINGS

Directions: After reading "Sky Woman" (Pupil's Edition, page 427), listen to someone retell this story. Rate that partner on his or her retelling by circling the number in the appropriate column that best describes the degree to which the reteller successfully included each item on the chart. (A rating of zero would mean that the reteller did not include the item at all; a rating of 1 would mean that the item was covered a little; a rating of 2 would mean that the item was covered in some detail but that something was incorrect or left out; and a rating of 3 would mean that the reteller accurately and completely covered the item in his or her retelling.) Then, switch roles. Be sure to complete the questions below the chart.

Retellings Rating Chart   Listener:_____

Does this retelling				
1. have a good beginning that explains when and where the story takes place?	0	1	2	3
2. tell the characters' names?	0	1	2	3
3. explain the main points of what happened?	0	1	2	3
4. keep those points in the correct order?	0	1	2	3
5. provide details?	0	1	2	3
6. make sense and sound organized?	0	1	2	3
7. tell what was the main problem in the story?	0	1	2	3
8. tell how the problem was solved?	0	1	2	3
9. connect the story to another story or to something in the reader's life?	0	1	2	3
10. provide any personal comments about the story?	0	1	2	3

Total Score: _____

Comments from the listener about the retelling: ....

....

Suggestions for the next retelling: ....

....

When the Earth Shakes

SKILL TRACKING CAUSE AND EFFECT | **STRATEGY** TEXT REFORMULATION

Directions: Choose one of the following passages from "When the Earth Shakes" (Pupil's Edition, page 435) to reformulate using the *If/Then* text pattern (*If A happens, then B happens; if B happens, then C happens . . .*). Then, begin writing your reformulation by completing the boxes below. Continue writing your reformulation on the back of this sheet. An example has been provided for you for number 1.

1. pages 436–437, paragraphs 14 through 16 (begins with "Seward was both a . . .")
2. page 437, paragraphs 17 through 22 (begins with "During that time . . .")
3. page 439, paragraphs 40 through 44 (begins with "When an earthquake . . .")

Example: *If Seward is the end of a rail line,*
               Then the train brings in a product, like oil.

If
_____
_____
_____

Then
_____
_____
_____

If
_____
_____
_____

Then
_____
_____
_____

If
_____
_____
_____

Then
_____
_____
_____

If
_____
_____
_____

Then
_____
_____
_____

from Survive the Savage Sea

SKILL ADJUSTING READING RATE | **STRATEGY** SAY SOMETHING

Part 1. Directions: Decide with a partner whether you will read "Survive the Savage Sea" (Pupil's Edition, page 444) silently or aloud. As you read, stop about every three or four paragraphs and take turns saying something about what you just read, including any comments you can make about adjusting your reading rate. In the chart below, write a check mark in the appropriate column for each type of comment you make.

Prediction	Comment	Question	Connection

Part 2. Directions: Think about the Say Something dialogue you had with your partner, and answer the following questions on the lines provided. You can continue your answers on the back of this page or on a separate sheet of paper.

1. If someone had been listening in on your Say Something dialogue, what would they have heard? Give a summary. ....
....

2. Did you answer any questions for your partner? Did your partner answer any questions for you? What were the questions? What questions remain unanswered? ....
....

3. Looking at your chart above, what type of comment did you make the most? Why do you think you made that type the most? ....
....

4. Think about the statements you made about adjusting your reading rate. How did the Say Something strategy help you? ....
....

5. If you do a Say Something again, how will you do it differently? ....
....
....

ELEMENTS OF LITERATURE

Antaeus

Directions: After you have finished reading "Antaeus," decide which text structure you will use to reformulate this selection: a newspaper article or an ABC-style story. Brainstorm ideas for your reformulation with two or three classmates. To help you get started, use the space within the graphic organizer to answer the following questions. Once you have finished brainstorming, write your reformulation on another sheet of paper.

1. What will your title be?
2. What will your purpose be? (to inform, to entertain, to persuade)
3. Who will your audience be? How will that affect your story?
4. Will it be serious or funny?
5. What details from the story do you want to include? What can you leave out?
6. What graphics or artwork will you include, if any?

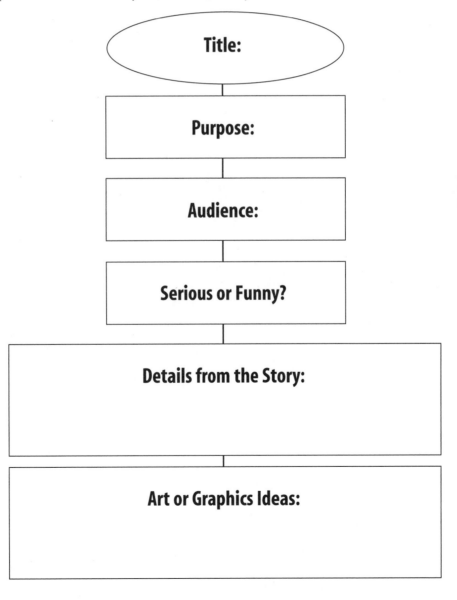

Title:

Purpose:

Audience:

Serious or Funny?

Details from the Story:

Art or Graphics Ideas:

ELEMENTS OF LITERATURE

The Origin of the Seasons

SKILL MONITORING COMPREHENSION | **STRATEGY** SAY SOMETHING

Part 1. Directions: Decide with a partner whether you will read "The Origin of the Seasons" (Pupil's Edition, page 500) silently or aloud. As you read, stop about every two or three paragraphs and take turns saying something about what you just read, including any comments you can make about monitoring your comprehension. In the chart below, write a check mark in the appropriate column for each type of comment you make.

Prediction	Comment	Question	Connection

Part 2. Directions: Think about the Say Something dialogue you had with your partner, and answer the following questions on the lines provided. You can continue your answers on the back of this page or on a separate sheet a paper.

1. If someone had been listening in on your Say Something dialogue, what would they have heard? Give a summary. ....

....

2. Did you answer any questions for your partner? Did your partner answer any questions for you? What were the questions? What questions remain unanswered? ....

....

3. Looking at your chart above, what type of comment did you make the most? Why do you think you made that type the most? ....

....

4. Think about the statements you made about monitoring your comprehension. How did the Say Something strategy help you? ....

....

5. If you do a Say Something again, how will you do it differently? ....

....

....

Orpheus, the Great Musician

SKILL SETTING PURPOSES FOR READING | **STRATEGY** STORY IMPRESSIONS

Part 1. Directions: Before reading "Orpheus, the Great Musician" (Pupil's Edition, page 513), read the key words in the following box. With a partner or on your own, think about how those words and phrases are similar to and different from one another. Then, write a Story Impression that shows how those words might be linked. Use the words and phrases in the exact order shown below. Continue your Story Impression on another sheet if necessary.

Key Words
musician Orpheus
↓
loves Eurydice
↓
wedding
↓
snake bite
↓
death
↓
underworld
↓
Orpheus follows
↓
beautiful music
↓
test
↓
failure
↓
death
↓
reunited

My Story Impression:

....
....
....
....
....
....
....
....
....
....
....
....
....

Part 2. Directions: After reading "Orpheus, the Great Musician," write a paragraph on the back of this sheet that explains how the connections between the key words in the selection differ from the connections between the key words in your Story Impression.

Echo and Narcissus

Prefixes

A *prefix* is one or more syllables added to the beginning of a word to create a new word with a meaning different from that of the original word.

Some Common Prefixes		
Prefix	**Meaning**	**Example**
fore–	before, front part of	forecast
in–	not	independent
inter–	between, among	interstate
mis–	badly, not, wrongly	mistaken
non–	not	nonnative
post–	after, following	postwar
pre–	before	preview
re–	back, again	replay
sub–	under, beneath	substandard
trans–	across, beyond	transcontinental
un–	not, reverse of	untrue

Suffixes

A *suffix* is one or more syllables added to the end of a word to create a new word. Often, adding a suffix changes both a word's part of speech and its meaning.

Some Common Suffixes		
Suffix	**Meaning**	**Example**
–able	able, likely	changeable
–dom	state, condition	freedom
–en	make, become	weaken
–er	having to do with	worker
–ful	full of, characteristic of	joyful
–fy	make, cause	justify
–ize	make, cause to be	realize
–less	without, lacking	tireless
–ly	characteristic of	gladly
–ment	result, action	agreement
–ness	quality, state	kindness
–or	one who	actor
–ive	nature or quality of	supportive
–ble	quality of	lovable
–ty	quality, state	cruelty
–y	condition, quality	dirty

The Flight of Icarus

SKILL MAKING GENERALIZATIONS | **STRATEGY** SKETCH TO STRETCH

Directions: After reading "The Flight of Icarus" (Pupil's Edition, page 530), sketch in the space below a symbolic picture that represents a generalization you made from reading the selection.

On the lines below, write an explanation of your sketch. Then, write the generalization you made that inspired the sketch.

I drew this because . . .

....

....

....

....

My generalization is that . . .

....

....

....

The Labors of Jermaine

1   As Jermaine looked at the week's work schedule posted beside the cash register, his smile quickly turned into a frown.

2   "Oh, no, Mr. Logan, I have to work Wednesday and Thursday nights this week? I asked for both nights off. I have a really big test in world history on Friday," complained Jermaine to his supervisor.

3   "Well, Kyle quit yesterday, and Brenda needs someone else to be here at night to help close the store. I'm sorry, Jermaine, but the store can't rely on anyone else to fill in like this. I can't hire someone that soon. You're one of my best employees, and it's because you're responsible that I'm asking you to help me out here," said Mr. Logan, the manager of the Sonic Sounds music store.

4   Jermaine really needed those two nights off. Since he had started working at the mall two months ago, he had hardly any time to study. In June, the school was sponsoring a one-week trip to Washington, D.C., and Jermaine really wanted to go. He had taken the job at the music store so that he could save up the money to go on the trip. The money he earned from working extra shifts would pay for the trip and leave him with enough spending money while he was in Washington. He thought he was set.

5   Besides having the money, each person had to be passing with a B average to be eligible. Unfortunately, Jermaine's averages in two of his classes turned from B's into low D's within a month. Jermaine knew that not having time to study for the test could lower his average to a point where it might be too low to bring up.

6   The next day at school, the counselor, Ms. Rodriguez, called Jermaine to the main office to talk about what was happening.

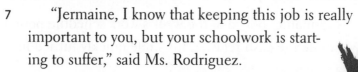

7   "Jermaine, I know that keeping this job is really important to you, but your schoolwork is starting to suffer," said Ms. Rodriguez.

8   "Well, I've been working so much lately to save up for that trip and everything that I haven't had too much time to study. I know what I need to do. I just need to ace the test this Friday in world history and I can bring my grade up, no problem. English is no sweat, either. I know I can pull them up, Ms. Rodriguez."

9   "Jermaine, even if you save up the money for the trip and even if you pull up the grades this time, what about next time? A shaky average could ruin your chances of going on this trip. A low overall average will also make it harder when you start thinking about college," Ms. Rodriguez said, looking straight into Jermaine's face. "Mr. Simmons has already told me that you might fail his class this grading period. He showed me your last test grade. A 59 won't cut it next time, not even a 70."

10   "But I can do it; just let me do it my way," said Jermaine.

11   Ms. Rodriguez took a long breath, and looked down at her desk. "I'm sorry, but if you won't quit your job, I can only ask that you really make your grades come first. Mr. Simmons said that if you don't get at least a B on your next test, then you'll fail his class. Make sure to study, Jermaine. I'd hate for you to miss the trip and end up taking summer school to make up the lost credit for world history. It would be a waste."

12   As Jermaine walked out of Ms. Rodriguez's office, the main office secretary, Mrs. Hobbs, asked, "Jermaine, do you mind taking this folder over to Mr. Simmons? He left this folder and these pages on the copy machine a few minutes ago, and they might be important."

13   "No problem," said Jermaine as Mrs. Hobbs handed him the folder.

14   Jermaine left the office and headed down the hallway to Mr. Simmons's classroom. As he walked, Jermaine tried to figure out what to do. He first thought about skipping a class to study for the test or just staying home on Friday and taking the makeup test later. Then he remembered that he already had 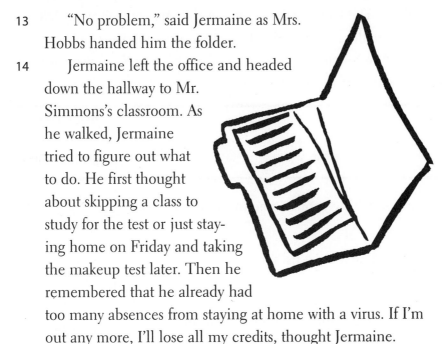 too many absences from staying at home with a virus. If I'm out any more, I'll lose all my credits, thought Jermaine.

15   Then he thought about calling in sick to work but realized that his supervisor would know he was lying. Jermaine didn't want to lose his job.

16   While thinking about all the choices before him, Jermaine glanced at the tab on the folder that he held in his hands. The tab was marked "test master." Suddenly Jermaine was curious. What if this is the actual test for this Friday? Should I look at it? If I just look at it, is it really cheating? It's not like looking at the answer key. All these thoughts raced through Jermaine's mind. He had a way out of this mess if he simply looked at the test master in the folder. But he had never done anything like this before. He personally thought cheating was a cop-out. He felt that people who cheated were both lazy and weak—too weak to live with making a low grade. He had never been really concerned about grades before and was pretty happy with B's and an occasional C. But if Jermaine didn't look at the test, he might fail the test, fail the class, and become ineligible for the Washington trip. Too much was on the line now.

The Labors of Jermaine

SKILL CONNECTING THROUGH YOUR EXPERIENCE | **STRATEGY** ANTICIPATION GUIDES

Part 1. Directions: Before reading the MiniRead "The Labors of Jermaine," read each of the following statements and decide if you agree or disagree with the statement. Mark an X in the appropriate blank in the *Before Reading* column. After reading, mark an X in the appropriate blank in the *After Reading* column to show whether or not your views were influenced by the text. Be prepared to explain your decisions.

BEFORE READING Agree / Disagree	Statement	AFTER READING Agree / Disagree
_____ / _____	1. It's okay to do something wrong sometimes for the right reasons.	_____ / _____
_____ / _____	2. You should be willing to take risks to get something you really want.	_____ / _____
_____ / _____	3. It's more important to think about the long-term effects of an action than the short-term gains.	_____ / _____

Part 2. Directions: Choose one of the Anticipation Guide statements above, and on the lines provided, describe how the statement you chose relates to the MiniRead.

....

....

....

....

Part 3. Directions: Look again at the Anticipation Guide. What kinds of things are similar or different between your own experiences and those of the character Jermaine in the MiniRead? Use the chart provided to explore those similarities and differences.

Jermaine's Experiences	My Own Experiences

ELEMENTS OF LITERATURE

The Labors of Hercules

SKILL CONNECTING THROUGH YOUR EXPERIENCE | **STRATEGY** ANTICIPATION GUIDES

Part 1. Directions: Before reading "The Labors of Hercules" (Pupil's Edition, page 541), read the statements below and decide if you agree or disagree with each statement. For each statement, mark an X in the appropriate blank in the *Before Reading* column. After reading, mark an X in the appropriate blank in the *After Reading* column to show whether or not your views were influenced by the selection.

BEFORE READING Agree / Disagree	Statement	AFTER READING Agree / Disagree
_____ / _____	1. Facing difficult problems makes you stronger.	_____ / _____
_____ / _____	2. As long as you do what you're supposed to do, it doesn't matter how you do it.	_____ / _____
_____ / _____	3. A hero is a person who is always brave and always gets the job done.	_____ / _____
_____ / _____	4. If you do something that is wrong, you can make up for it by doing good deeds.	_____ / _____
_____ / _____	5. People who do very bad things, no matter how much they regret doing them, should never become role models or heroes.	_____ / _____

Part 2. Directions: Find where each statement in Part 1 is discussed in "The Labors of Hercules." Does the information in the selection support your belief or make you rethink your belief? Complete the chart below, writing what "The Labors of Hercules" says about each statement.

What "The Labors of Hercules" says about the statement

1. ....
....

2. ....
....

3. ....
....

4. ....
....

5. ....

King Midas and the Golden Touch

SKILL USING PRIOR KNOWLEDGE | **STRATEGY** ANTICIPATION GUIDES

Part 1. Directions: Before reading "King Midas and the Golden Touch" (Pupil's Edition, page 559), read each of the statements below and decide if you agree or disagree with the statement. For each statement, mark your choice in the appropriate blank. Be prepared to explain your decisions.

BEFORE READING Agree / Disagree	Statement	AFTER READING Agree / Disagree
_____ / _____	1. People who have money are happier than people who are poor.	_____ / _____
_____ / _____	2. People should just be happy with what they have.	_____ / _____
_____ / _____	3. Money leads to problems.	_____ / _____
_____ / _____	4. Powerful people are people who have a lot of money.	_____ / _____
_____ / _____	5. People shouldn't want a lot of power.	_____ / _____

Part 2. Directions: Find where each statement in Part 1 is discussed in "King Midas and the Golden Touch." Does the information in the selection support your belief or make you rethink your belief? Complete the chart below, writing what "King Midas and the Golden Touch" says about each statement.

What "King Midas and the Golden Touch" says about the statement

1. ....
....

2. ....
....

3. ....
....

4. ....
....

5. ....
....

ELEMENTS OF LITERATURE

Aesop's Fables

SKILL IDENTIFYING A TEXT'S PURPOSE | **STRATEGY** TEXT REFORMULATION

Part 1. Directions: After reading the Aesop's Fables on pages 567–573 of the Pupil's Edition, choose one fable to reformulate in two ways:

- Reformulate the fable once with a text structure that would encourage readers to read with the purpose of gaining information.
- Reformulate the fable a second time with a text structure that would encourage readers to read with the purpose of enjoying the story.

Write one reformulation in the space below and the other on the back of this page. Continue your reformulations on another sheet if necessary.

....

....

....

....

....

....

....

....

....

....

....

....

Part 2. Directions: After you have completed your reformulations, exchange them with a partner. Have the partner read your reformulations and fill in the information for blanks 1, 2, and 3. **You** circle the correct choice for number 4.

1. My name is ....

2. I read the reformulations and think .... is the reformulation that encourages reading for information.

3. .... is the reformulation that encourages reading for enjoyment.

4. My partner's interpretation of the purposes for the above reformulations (matched/did not match) my interpretation.

ELEMENTS OF LITERATURE

Aschenputtel

SKILL DETERMINING THE MAIN IDEA | **STRATEGY** MOST IMPORTANT WORD

Part 1. Directions: After reading "Aschenputtel" (Pupil's Edition, page 593), look back through the story and choose what you consider to be the most important word. Then, complete the following statements on the lines provided.

1. The most important word in this story is ....

2. List several reasons for choosing this word. Be sure that your reasons are supported with examples directly from the selection.
I chose this word because

....

....

....

....

....

3. Using the most important word I chose from this selection, I now think that the main idea of

this story is ....

....

....

(Be sure to use your most important word as you complete the statement.)

Part 2. Directions: In the drawing below, write your main idea in the body of the dove. Then, in each wing of the dove, write down your supporting details or examples from "Aschenputtel" that back up your main idea.

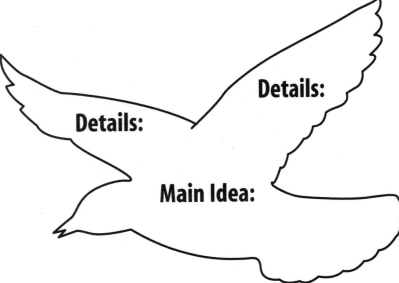

Details:

Details:

Main Idea:

ELEMENTS OF LITERATURE

The Algonquin Cinderella / Yeh-Shen

SKILL COMPARING TEXTS | **STRATEGY** COMPARISON GRID

Part 1. Directions: In the spaces below, identify each of the following characters for each selection. The first line has been completed for you.

Character	"The Algonquin Cinderella"	"Yeh-Shen"
Helper-type person	Example: *middle sister, The Invisible One's sister*	Example: *old sage, fish bones*
Cinderella character	....	....
Prince character	....	....
Cinderella's enemy	....	....

Part 2. Directions: Using one colored pencil for "The Algonquin Cinderella" and a different colored pencil for "Yeh-Shen," indicate where you would place each character by placing each character's name or initials in the square that indicates his or her amount of kindness and wisdom.

	very kind	kind	neither	mean	very mean
very foolish					
foolish					
neither					
wise					
very wise					

Part 3. Directions: Answer the following questions on the back of this sheet. Refer to your grid.

1. Which characters from the two stories are the most similar? Which are the most different? Explain.

2. How did rating the characters help you see their differences and/or similarities?

ELEMENTS OF LITERATURE

Seeing Is Believing

1   Alex still couldn't believe what she had seen. She had
    been minding her own business, dusting supplies in
    the back room of her father's small grocery store. She
had moved a carton of paper plates to one side to dust behind
it, and through the opening she could see the cash register.

2   There at the register was Bobbi, Alex's co-worker and best
friend. Bobbi was closing the cash drawer with one hand and
shoving a twenty-dollar bill into her pocket with the other!

3   Alex hurriedly replaced the carton and leaned against the
wall. She felt dazed and could hardly breathe. She had begged
her father to hire Bobbi, and this was the thanks she got!

4   How could I have misjudged Bobbi so much? Alex
thought. I must not have seen what I thought I saw.

5   But she had to admit that she had, in fact, seen it. Her father
would have to be told. But first, Alex decided, she would talk to
Bobbi. Maybe Bobbi would have an explanation, though Alex
had to admit that she herself couldn't think of one.

6   Every day after the store closed, Alex's father counted out
the money in the register and took it to the bank, leaving the
clerks to clean up. Alex decided that she would talk with
Bobbi as soon as they were alone. In the meantime, she
would keep an eye on the cash register.

7   The rest of the day was agony for Alex. One minute, she
was so mad at Bobbi that she wished they had never met. The
next minute, she was sure that Bobbi had an explanation,
which only made her feel bad for doubting her best friend.

8   Finally, Alex's father locked the front door and started
counting the money in the cash register. Ten minutes later,
he pulled on his jacket and headed for the back door.

9   "See you at Pete's Diner," he said to Alex.

10   Alex had completely forgotten! Her dad was treating her to
dinner that evening to mark the first anniversary of the day
she started working at the grocery store. Now that would be
ruined, all because of Bobbi.

11   As soon as her father left, Alex turned
to Bobbi and said, "We have to talk."

12   "Sure, Alex," said Bobbi. "What's up?"

13   "I saw what you did," Alex said.

14   "What are you talking about?" asked Bobbi.

15   "I saw you take twenty dollars out of the cash register," Alex said firmly.

16   "Oh that," said Bobbi calmly. "I was just—"

17   Then Bobbi paused. She seemed to be realizing something.

18   "Oh, I know what you think you saw," stated Bobbi. "I can understand why you would be angry. But you should talk to your dad before you jump to any conclusions."

19   "I'm not jumping to any conclusions. I don't have to jump. You made everything very clear," Alex said.

20   "But don't you want—?" Bobbi said before Alex cut her off.

21   "All I want is for you to put the money back and get out of here."

22   "But Alex, we're friends. Friends trust friends," said Bobbi.

23   "Well, I can't trust you, so maybe we aren't friends," Alex said.

24   Bobbi stared at her, shook her head, picked up her backpack, and headed toward the door. She said, "You are going to feel like a fool."

25   "At least I'll never feel like a thief!"

26   Bobbi felt the sting of tears as she let the door slam behind her.

27   Later, Alex walked two blocks to Pete's Diner where she found her father in a corner booth.

28   Alex told him what she had seen and said. She expected her father to be angry, but he just sat there smiling.

29   "I don't see what's so funny," Alex exclaimed.

30   "But I do," her father replied, placing a small flat box on the table. Alex unwrapped it and found inside a new CD box set she had been planning to buy once she saved up a little more money.

31   "I had Bobbi pick it up for me on her way to work," he said. "It's for working hard at the store. Bobbi paid for it, and I didn't quite have enough cash to repay her, so I told her to get it out of the cash register."

32   "Oh," said Alex softly. Then her face darkened. "I've made a terrible mistake."

Seeing Is Believing

SKILL SUMMARIZING | **STRATEGY** SOMEBODY WANTED BUT SO

Directions: After you have read the MiniRead "Seeing Is Believing," complete the following chart by making a series of statements, one statement for each character. After completing the chart, use the back of this sheet to write a summary of the MiniRead.

Somebody	Wanted	But	So
Alex's father			

Then

Alex			

Then

Bobbi			

Then

Alex			

ELEMENTS OF LITERATURE

Oni and the Great Bird

Directions: After you have finished reading "Oni and the Great Bird" (Pupil's Edition, page 629), complete each of the following Somebody Wanted But So statements. Then, answer the question below the chart.

Somebody	Wanted	But	So
1. The people of Ajo			
2. Oni			
3. Oni killed the bird and	wanted to claim		

4. Which statement gives you the best summary for "Oni and the Great Bird"? What makes that statement the best?

....

....

....

Master Frog

Part 1. Directions: Study the following words and phrases from "Master Frog" and then arrange them into the appropriate categories shown in the chart below. After placing words into categories, complete the following Probable Passage. Then read "Master Frog" on page 638 of the Pupil's Edition. After reading the story, complete Part 2 below.

Words and Phrases to Sort

the frog becomes a prince   Princess Kien Tien

they live happily ever after   saved by Jade Emperor and Dragon King

he is a frog   sisters

jealousy   kill Princess Kien Tien

Master Frog   Vietnam

Categories for Sorting Words and Phrases

Setting	Character(s)	Problem(s)	Solution(s)	Ending

Probable Passage to Complete

The story mainly takes place in [1]........................... . [2]........................... is the main character

whose problem is that [3]........................... . He convinces [4]...........................to marry him and

then because of their love [5]........................... . Princess Kien's [6]...........................are filled with

[7]........................... and plot to [8]........................... . But that problem is solved when Master Frog

and Princess Kien Tien are [9]........................... . At the end, [10]........................... .

Part 2. Directions: Review your Probable Passage on the back of this sheet. Explain how your Probable Passage differed from "Master Frog." Be sure to give specific examples.

ELEMENTS OF LITERATURE

ADDITIONAL PRACTICE

Strategy: It Says ... I Say

Question	It Says ... + (What the text says)	I Say ... = (My thoughts)	And So ... (My inference)

Strategy: It Says ... I Say

Question	It Says ... + (What the text says)	I Say ... = (My thoughts)	And So ... (My inference)

Strategy: Say Something

In the chart below, write a check mark in the appropriate column for each type of "Say Something" comment you make.

Prediction	Comment	Question	Connection

Think about the Say Something dialogue you had with your partner, and answer the following questions on the lines provided.

1. If someone had been listening in on your Say Something dialogue, what would they have heard? Give a summary. ....

....

2. Did you answer any questions for your partner? Did your partner answer any questions for you? What were the questions? What questions remain unanswered? ....

....

3. Looking at your chart above, what type of comment did you make the most? Why do you think you made that type the most? ....

....

4. If you do a Say Something again, how will you do it differently? ....

....

....

ELEMENTS OF LITERATURE

Strategy: Somebody Wanted But So

Somebody	Wanted	But	So

ELEMENTS OF LITERATURE

Strategy: Somebody Wanted But So

Somebody	Wanted	But	So

Strategy: Think-Aloud

Think-Aloud Tally Sheet   **Listener:**_____

Think-Aloud Comments	Tally
Making predictions	
Picturing the text	
Making comparisons	
Identifying problems	
Fixing problems	
Making a comment	